This book was inspired by my beloved Tasmanian Labradoodle. Thank you to all of the clients that have worked with me. They've reinforced, time and time again, the importance of repairing the child-parent/caregiver relationship after a rupture.

Licensed exclusively to Cardinal House Press
P.O. BOX HM 2298
Hamilton, Bermuda HMJX

Text copyright © 2018 Dr. Tina J. Arorash
Illustration copyright © 2018 Aleksandra Szmidt

Printed by CreateSpace, An Amazon.com Company

ISBN-13: 978-0999806807 (Cardinal House Press)
ISBN-10: 0999806807

Oops – To Feeling Good

It all started one ordinary Tuesday evening.

Tass was feeling very tired after returning home from a long day's work.

As soon as Tass arrived home from work, she and Boris immediately went outside to play.

Boris loves everything! He is a very enthusiastic and curious puppy.
He can play for hours!

Boris is never ready to stop
playing when Tass tells him that
it's time to go inside for dinner.

She calmly waits for Boris. Eventually he joins her inside the kitchen, where she is usually making dinner. As soon as his nose catches a whiff of the roasted chicken, he starts his wacka-doodle nightly dance.

After dinner, Tass rested on the steps. Boris wondered, what's wrong with Tass? Tass said, "Boris, will you clean the kitchen tonight? I am VERY tired."

"What a sweet boy!" she said, while stroking Boris's fleecy ears. It's the last thing that she remembered before falling asleep on the steps.

When Tass woke up, awake but still groggy, she looked down at her wet slippers. Lo and behold, you'll never guess what else she saw!

Take a guess.

But this time, when she looked down at her slippers, she noticed that there were bubbles on her slippers. *BUBBLES!?!* Where did the bubbles come from?

She felt worried. Just then, all of a sudden, she felt butterflies in her stomach. It felt like they were dancing inside of her tummy.

Her worry turned to anger. She angrily said, "BORIS, where are you?" She had a strong feeling that he was getting into trouble and making a big mess AGAIN. He's such a curious pup and often gets into trouble when he's quiet.

"Oh Boris! What now?" she said in a frustrated voice.

She almost broke into a run – rushing around the house, looking in his usual hiding and nesting spots. But this time, there was no Boris.

When Tass reached the bottom of the steps - SWOOSH - her foot was submerged in soapy water. She squealed, "Oh my!!!"

And then, a miracle happened. A miracle is a wonderful event that people say is caused by God.

You'll never guess what she saw. She didn't believe it herself. She thought, I've officially gone crazy! No one is EVER going to believe THIS story. At the end of the kitchen, there stood, have you guessed yet?

She turned her head and saw
Boris standing up at the kitchen
sink washing dishes! Bubbles were
everywhere - an explosion of
bubbles!

Boris was having the time of his life! He was having a blast. He FINALLY was able to play with the bubbles and water like Tass usually did. He longed for a turn. And today she finally gave him permission. Whoo hoooo – to clean the dishes.

Tass shouted, "Boris, get down!"

She was really scared, but it sounded like she was really mad. He looked at her confused, which then made her mad. She thought..you know that I'm upset with you! Couldn't he tell that she was upset with him?

She wanted him to jump down from the sink immediately because he was making a terrible mess, everywhere! The situation was getting worse because he couldn't reach the faucet to turn off the water.

Boris was so confused. He thought, how could she be so mad at me? She asked me to clean the kitchen. I just did what she asked me to do.

Boris felt overwhelmed by how mad Tass seemed. He was torn up inside. He wanted to be comforted by Tass. He needed her help to feel better.

Who was going to help him with his big feelings?

Tass was very upset with herself for falling asleep and for not watching over Boris more carefully. She panicked when she called out to Boris and he didn't come like he usually does.

Her brain thought the worse. She was afraid and then she automatically became angry. She was afraid that Boris could be hurt by something in the sink like a sharp knife.

Boris looked at Tass and knew that he was in deep trouble. It was the tone of her voice. He **KNEW** she was upset with him, but **he had no idea why**. Her reddened skin, he knew what that meant too.

He remembered the last time that he had seen that reddened face, it was after he had jumped up on the kitchen counter and eaten her supper. Just then, he heard a loud noise, coming out of Tass. It scared him.

She was laughing hysterically. She thought, it could be much, much worse. There could be broken dishes everywhere. Boris wasn't hurt in the confusion.

Once she realized that Boris was safe, she was able to see the humor in it. Boris looked like he thought he was going to be in serious trouble. He looked at Tass in a sad and confused way.

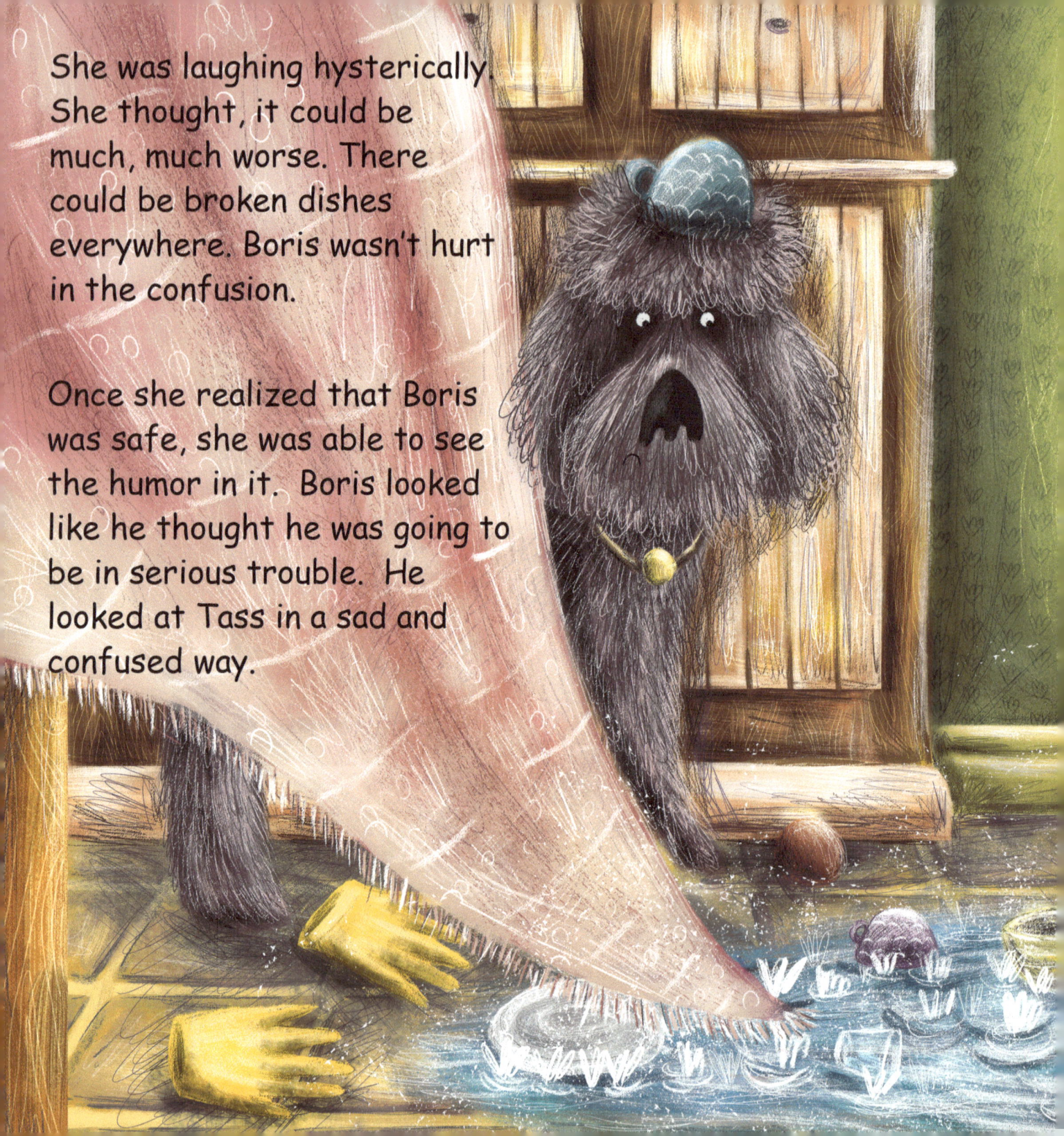

She immediately went over to Boris and bent down beside him. She thought, **that obedient and loving dog!**

Boris wasn't sure what was going to happen next? What is Tass going to do?

She reached out and gave him
a loving cuddle. It felt
REALLY good.

Boris let out a big sigh of relief, which sounded like a gigantic yawn.

He thought, Tass isn't mad at me, though somewhat surprised. And just like that his heart rate calmed and he could breathe more easily again.

Whew!

She removed the sudsy gloves from Boris' paws, dried him off and then settled him upstairs.

She said, "I'm so sorry for putting you at risk. Things could've been much worse. I shouldn't have asked you to do adult things because things could go wrong."

"Things could happen that you wouldn't be able to understand or know how to fix. I'm so sorry. Please forgive me Boris. Tass isn't mad at you.

You didn't do anything wrong."

He was so relieved that
they were good again. He
really didn't feel good
whenever Tass was upset
with him.

It hurt his heart a lot and
it made him feel very sad.

Tass said, "I didn't expect you to understand what I was asking. I was just being silly!"

Tass definitely learned her lesson that evening. She thought, I'll never ask Boris to do things like that ever again.

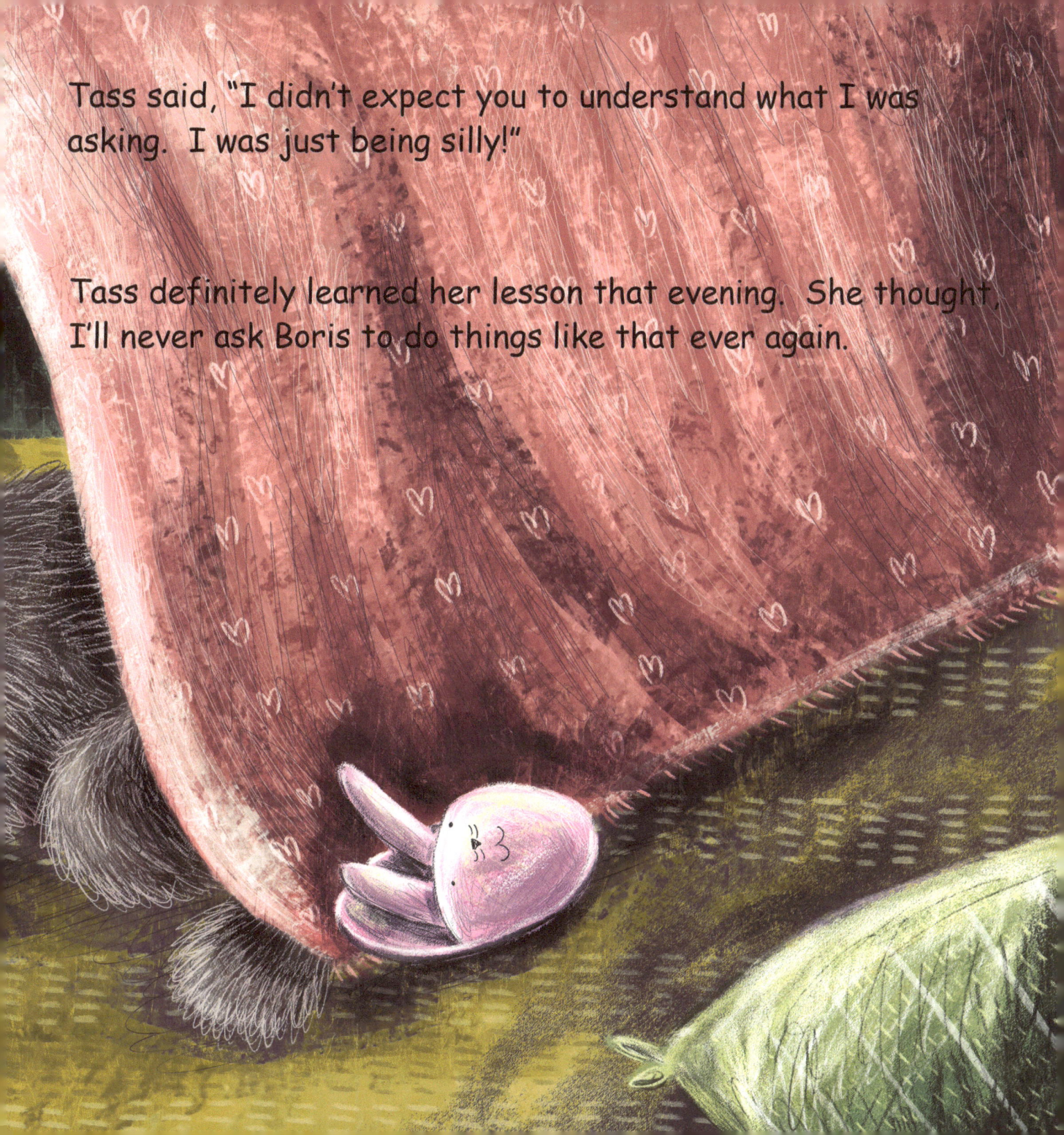

A week later, Granny came over for a visit, with Angus.

Granny was feeling very tired when it was time for her to leave.

You'll never guess what words she spoke to Boris, as she leaned in to give him a goodbye snuggle.   Have you guessed? She said, "Boris, Granny's tired, will you drive Granny home?"

Note to Caregivers/Parents:

Oops – To Feeling Good is a comedic and heartwarming story about how misunderstandings often ensue between children and the adults in their lives (for example, when a child has misunderstood the directive or has missed the context of the adult's request). This book displays how both adult and child might misread the other's social cues and/or intention(s) – such as, voice volume, body language, tone of voice, verbal request, etc. It teaches the importance of the need to repair the relationship once it has temporarily gone off the rails.

Modern day family life is moving at a fast pace and this story reminds us about the importance of connection and the indescribable necessity of feeling "felt" by one's loved one(s). The goal of this story is that it will encourage caregivers to spend more time listening to a child's feelings rather than rushing to fix the behaviour or emotion. It is so important to slow down and take the time to understand the child's feeling state. It also aids the child in understanding their feeling states.

It is important to accurately understand the emotional state of the other in order to facilitate healthy secure attachments. For the parent/caregiver, the goal is to increase their reflective functioning capacity – to recognize their child's feeling state as separate from their own and to interpret the child's feelings accurately. This in turn aids the child in better understanding their own feeling state which can often times be overwhelming to them given that they may be experiencing the intensity of their emotions for the first time and may not readily be able to identify the feelings and then verbally express them to their caregiver.

Moreover, it is important that the parent/caregivers overtly assume responsibility for situations that go wrong when its' not inherently the child's fault to diminish their tendency to assume the burden of responsibility. This book can provide a springboard for child and caregiver to discuss times when they have experienced similar situations when they misunderstood one another's feelings or intentions.

Note for Children:

While reading **Oops – To Feeling Good**, it may be helpful to ask children questions and/or guide them while they view the illustrations and/or after they have read the story, asking questions, such as:

🐾 How do you think Boris feels?

🐾 Have you ever felt like Boris?

🐾 How do you feel in your body when you are worried, scared or mad? [It may be helpful to provide a menu of choices if the child gets stuck – for example, feeling hot, sweaty hands, heart racing, butterflies in tummy, trouble breathing, etc.]

🐾 Have you ever gotten into trouble? How was it fixed/resolved?

🐾 Do you ever feel stuck when a situation goes wrong?

🐾 What do you like best about Boris? Least?

🐾 What do you like best about Tass? Least?

About the Author
Dr. Tina J. Arorash

Tina enjoys a thriving child and family clinical practice in the archipelago of Bermuda. She received her Ph.D. from Columbia University.

About the Illustrator
Aleksandra Szmidt

Her love of drawing plants and animals is attributed to her landscape architecture studies. However, she prefers to design magical things often detached from reality.

Center For Family Development

Arthur Becker-Weidman, PhD
Web Site: www.Center4FamilyDevelop.com

5820 Main St., Suite 406, Caldwell Bldg.,
Williamsville, NY 14221
41 Madison Avenue, Suite 3130,
New York, NY 10010

phone: 716-636-6243

Phone: 646-389-6550

Fax: 716-636-6243

E-mail:AWeidman@Concentric.net

September 11, 2017

REVIEW OF "Oops – To Feeling Good," by Dr. Tina J. Arorash

This delightful story, seemingly so innocuous, is full of wonderful messages for both parents and children about emotions and intentions gone awry and then repaired. As I read the story a second time I am struck by the clear prose and the messages conveyed by the prose. This is a book that all parents of toddlers and young children should be reading with their children. This also happens to be a book that I expect to use and recommend to parents of the families I treat because it brings up such important topics about how to express anger, disappointment, love, and other emotions. Finally, as a terrific added bonus, the "Note to Parents," and the "Note to Children," provide guidance about the story and how to begin a conversation with each other about the story. This truly is a ***must read*** book.

Sincerely,

Arthur Becker-Weidman, Ph.D.
Diplomate, American College of Forensic Examiners
Diplomate, American Board of Psychological Specialties in Forensic Psychology
Diplomate, American Board of Psychological Examiners in Child Psychology
Registered Clinician, Association for the Treatment and Training in the Attachment of Children
Certified Therapist, Consultant, & Trainer, Dyadic Developmental Psychotherapy Institute
Certified Psychotherapist, Consultant, & Trainer, Attachment Focused Treatment Institute

REGISTERED AGENCY: ASSOCIATION FOR TREATMENT AND TRAINING IN THE ATTACHMENT OF CHILDREN,
COALITION OF ADOPTION AND FOSTER FAMILY AGENCIES,
CERTIFIED ATTACHMENT-FOCUSED TREATMENT ORGANIZATION

www.ingramcontent.com/pod-product-compliance
Lightning Source LLC
Chambersburg PA
CBHW060853270326
41934CB00002B/122